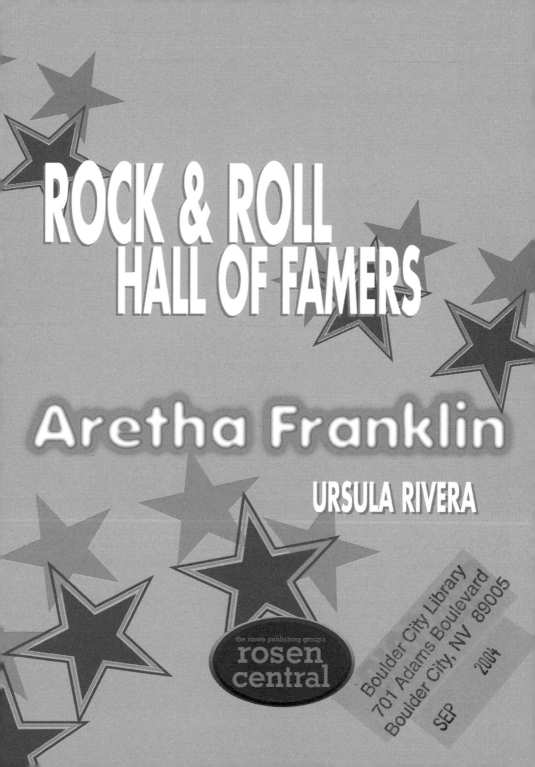

ROCK & ROLL
HALL OF FAMERS

Aretha Franklin

URSULA RIVERA

the rosen publishing group's
rosen
central

To Ava Gueudinot, from her soul sister

Published in 2003 by The Rosen Publishing Group, Inc.
29 East 21st Street, New York, NY 10010

First Edition

Library of Congress Cataloging-in-Publication Data

Rivera, Ursula.
Aretha Franklin / by Ursula Rivera.—1st ed.
   p. cm. — (Rock & roll hall of famers)
Includes discography (p.   ), bibliographical references (p.   ), and index.
Summary: Explores the life of the artist who has won more Grammy Awards than any other female singer and who, along with her success in soul and gospel music, has been inducted into the Rock and Roll Hall of Fame.
ISBN 0-8239-3639-2 (lib. bdg.)
1. Franklin, Aretha—Juvenile literature. 2. Soul musicians—United States—Biography—Juvenile literature. [1. Franklin, Aretha. 2. Singers. 3. Soul music. 4. African Americans—Biography. 5. Women—Biography.] I. Title. II. Series.
ML3930.F68 R58 2002
782.421644'092—dc21

2001007609

Manufactured in the United States of America

CONTENTS

Introduction   5

1. Child of the Gospel   8

2. The First Recordings   28

3. Success at Atlantic   42

4. Voice of Her Time   56

5. Down but Never Out   70

6. New Directions   88

Selected Discography   104

Glossary   105

To Find Out More   107

For Further Reading   108

Index   109

Aretha Franklin, the Queen of Soul, is a living legend whose career has spanned hits in gospel, R & B, soul, and pop music.

Introduction

Aretha Franklin. For many people, just hearing her name brings powerful music to mind: "Respect," "Think," "Amazing Grace." Aretha's song titles say everything about the woman herself. Her songs uplift, entertain, and inspire people from all walks of life. Her music played a powerful part during a time of change and struggle in American history.

The music Aretha has performed throughout her life has been shaped by her own experiences. It's proof of Aretha's incredible talent that her gospel roots made her not only the "Queen of Soul," but also an artist who could perform blues, jazz, hip-hop and even opera. There really is nothing she can't sing. She has used her voice for nearly fifty years to inspire her fans, and to sing the stories that so many people can relate to.

Aretha's life has been an amazing journey. As a shy young woman she idolized the great gospel singers Clara Ward and Mahalia Jackson. Aretha grew up to become a great gospel singer herself. She also grew up to become a confident, successful, and independent African American woman.

Aretha has lived through terrible tragedy. She has supported beloved members of her family through sickness and death, while struggling with her own grief. She is the daughter of a powerful preacher, the sister of songwriters and singers, and the mother of four talented sons.

Aretha's fans come from every walk of life. She has performed for kings and queens, presidents and first ladies, and millions of people of every race, gender, and age. All of her fans are united by the power of her voice. Aretha sings songs they care about, take comfort in, and that get their feet dancing.

Aretha Franklin's background in gospel music carried over into success in many other musical styles.

Aretha has been recognized as a diva. She's been inducted into the Rock and Roll Hall of Fame. She's won more Grammy Awards than any other female performer. Aretha Franklin is truly a living legend!

Child of the Gospel

Aretha Louise Franklin was born on March 25, 1942, in Memphis, Tennessee, Her father was Reverend Clarence LaVaughn Franklin (known as C.L.), a preacher in the Baptist Church. Aretha's mother was Barbara Siggers Franklin, a gospel singer and talented pianist. Aretha had an older sister, Erma, and two older brothers, Vaughn and Cecil. Later, her younger sister, Carolyn, was born.

The Daughter of a Preacher Man

C.L. Franklin grew up in Mississippi. After leaving high school in the tenth grade, he began working as a sharecropper, traveling seasonally to pick cotton and other crops. Even as a young man, C.L. was known for his powerful speaking voice and his ability to inspire people with his words. He started preaching when he was seventeen years old. Before long, he was able to make a living as a preacher and he settled briefly in Clarksdale, Mississippi.

Before Aretha was born, the Franklin family moved to Memphis, Tennessee, where her father attended LeMoyne College. Though he had been raised in a very religious household, C.L. Franklin's experiences traveling and attending college expanded his horizons. He appreciated many different points of view, and he loved the arts, especially music. Reverend Franklin's love of artistic expression was passed on to his children, especially his daughters, who were all musically gifted.

Soon after Aretha was born, the Franklins moved to Buffalo, New York, where her father became the pastor of a Baptist church. Aretha's mother began working as a nurse's aide. Reverend Franklin's reputation as a powerful preacher continued to grow, and soon he was receiving job offers from many other cities.

When Aretha was two years old, Reverend Franklin accepted a position as the pastor of the New Bethel Baptist Church in Detroit, Michigan. Though he didn't know it yet, Reverend Franklin's career with New Bethel would become enormously successful. His success as a minister would bring thousands of new members to his church and he would be influential in the growing civil rights movement. As Reverend Franklin's career grew, however, his marriage was falling apart.

When Aretha was six years old, her parents separated. Barbara Franklin moved back to Buffalo with Aretha's brother, Vaughn. The other four children remained in Detroit with Reverend Franklin. In later years it was reported that Barbara Franklin abandoned her family, but

Aretha denied this in her autobiography. "It is an absolute lie that our mother abandoned us," Aretha wrote. "She never lost sight of her children or her parenting responsibilities—and her visits continued regularly." Each year, Aretha and the other children would spend the summers with their mother in Buffalo.

A Good Life in Detroit

In the early 1950s, Detroit was attracting

Did You Know?

Aretha Franklin's got a lot of soul! She is known as the Queen of Soul. Bessie Smith was Queen of the Blues, Mahalia Jackson was the Queen of Gospel, and Dinah Washington was just The Queen!

many black families from the South who moved
north to enjoy a higher standard of living.
Because of his success in ministering, Reverend
Franklin was able to provide a good living for his
children in Detroit. Aretha and her family lived
in a large house that was provided by the church.
The family had a housekeeper, something that
was unusual for a black family at the time. Their
neighborhood included other successful black
business people and their families.

Aretha attended Alger Elementary School and
was a good student. When she wasn't at school,
Aretha spent many hours teaching herself to play
the piano. By listening to jazz records, Aretha
taught herself to play along. Aretha's sisters Erma
and Carolyn were also talented piano players.

Reverend Franklin was proud of all three of
his daughters. He recognized their talents and
encouraged them to sing in church. Aretha and
her sisters performed in the junior choir at New
Bethel Baptist Church. It was in the junior choir
that people first began to notice Aretha's
powerful voice.

From the moment she was born, Aretha had been exposed to people who used their voices to communicate in powerful ways. Her mother was a gifted gospel singer. Her father used his voice to preach moving sermons in church. Reverend Franklin's career as a preacher was so successful that he began recording his sermons and releasing them on records. During his lifetime, more than seventy of Reverend Franklin's sermons were released on record.

Tragedy Strikes

When Aretha was ten years old, her mother died of a heart attack. Aretha and her brothers and sisters attended the funeral in Buffalo. Reverend Franklin remained a strong parent throughout their lives, but the Franklin children were heartbroken. Nothing could replace the loss of their beloved mother.

Fortunately, Aretha and the others had many female influences in Detroit. Reverend Franklin's mother, whom the children called Big Mama, lived with the family for a time. Reverend

A Brief History of Gospel Music

Gospel music has its roots in the African American spirituals that were sung by slaves beginning in the 1700s. Slaves were brought from Africa to America by force, and were converted to Christianity by their slave owners. Often the owners required slaves to attend church, usually in separate services that were held only for slaves. During the eighteenth century it was common for a preacher to lead a congregation in a hymn by singing the song one line at a time—the congregation would sing each line back to the preacher. This was known as lining out or raising a hymn.

As the slaves performed backbreaking and monotonous work day in and day out, they began to raise their voices in song. Some slave spirituals began as variations on Christian hymns, but over the years many original compositions were created. Most of these songs were passed down orally, or by word of mouth, since very few slaves had access to methods of writing music. The American slaves were living lives of hopelessness, extreme physical pain, and brutality. Singing was a way of coping with awful circumstances. Their spirituals sang of a beautiful life after death as a way to inspire and uplift each other.

Following the Civil War, many slaves moved north, and their songs and traditions moved with them. Some African American churches, like the Pentecostal and Holiness denominations, incorporated lining out with "holy

A Brief History of Gospel Music

(continued)

dances" in which churchgoers would wave their arms, stomp their feet, or even faint with excitement when they "got the spirit." Other denominations, like the Baptists, were more conservative and did not think this behavior was appropriate.

In 1921, however, many of these divisions were blurred by the publication of *Gospel Pearls*. *Gospel Pearls* was a collection of hymns and spirituals that was adopted by many different denominations. The popularity of the music grew throughout countless African American churches, and touring gospel vocalists continued to spread this unique musical tradition.

Franklin's partner, Lola Moore, also lived with the Franklins. Though they never married, Moore lived with the reverend for many years. When the relationship ended, the Franklin children again lost a woman who was very important to them. Aretha's brother Cecil ran after the taxi that took Moore away, crying and begging her to come back to them.

Getting Up to Sing

Reverend Franklin was aware of how gifted young Aretha was, but he did not push her to perform as a child. He encouraged her to continue her piano studies. He gave her time to become aware of the power of her voice. Aretha was a shy girl, and though she loved music, she was not immediately drawn to performing.

Aretha had sung for several years as part of the junior choir at New Bethel Baptist Church. Eventually she began performing as a soloist. Even as a child, Aretha's voice was remarkable. Her voice sounded much older than her years, and people were deeply moved by the way she sang gospel music. Aretha soon found that she could put aside her shyness when she was on stage. She found self-esteem and power in the way that audiences responded to her. She became more confident each time she performed.

Influenced by the Best

During her childhood, Aretha was exposed to some of the greatest gospel singers of the time. Many of them were friends of her father's. Aretha was well acquainted with Mahalia Jackson, Sam Cooke and the Soul Stirrers, and Clara Ward and the Ward Singers. Many of these performers were experiencing "crossover" success. Jackson and Ward were successfully introducing white audiences to the power of gospel music. Cooke would soon have enormous success singing popular music.

Aretha's own style as a child was most influenced by Clara Ward, whose dramatic performances were legendary. The Ward Singers were famous for their theatrical style. Rather than wear choir robes, which were common costumes for gospel singers, the Ward Singers performed in eye-catching dresses and elaborate wigs. Clara Ward was an excellent piano player and an equally good singer who was best known for her upbeat versions of "How I Got Over" and "The Old Landmark."

Gospel singer and soul pioneer Sam Cooke was a big influence on a young Aretha Franklin.

There is little doubt that Ward's flair made an impression on young Aretha, who later performed in some outrageous outfits herself!

Ward deeply loved young Aretha, and Aretha looked up to her as a role model. Ward once wrote of Aretha, "My baby Aretha doesn't know how good she is. Doubts self. Some day—to the moon! I love that girl."

Aretha had a huge crush on Sam Cooke—as did many thousands of young women. Cooke was a well-known gospel singer with his group, the Soul Stirrers. After leaving the Soul Stirrers, Cooke began a successful solo career in pop music. His song "You Send Me" was a huge hit with both white and black audiences.

Like many young singers, Aretha tried imitating the styles and sounds that appealed to her. She imitated the flair of Clara Ward and the smooth vocals of Sam Cooke so well that Reverend Franklin told Aretha to focus more on expressing herself. She took her father's advice, which paid off in a big way!

On the Road

To help support his large family, Reverend Franklin began touring with his own gospel revue. The revue featured a dramatic sermon by Reverend Franklin and several musical numbers. When Aretha was fourteen years old, her father invited her to perform as part of the show. Her time on the road exposed Aretha to many

Aretha, now established as an international star, belts out a tune in January 1972.

different aspects of life. She was positively influenced by her exposure to new people and places. She continued to encounter some of the best gospel performers of the time.

Life on the road had drawbacks, too. Aretha was now traveling in a world of adults, with very few people her own age. Unlike her privileged upbringing in Detroit, there were many

Aretha Franklin speaks at a press conference on March 26, 1973.

places the revue traveled where they faced racism. Sometimes the performers would have to drive miles out of their way in order to find a restaurant that would serve the black performers.

Ultimately, the tour was another way that Reverend Franklin kept Aretha's mind open to many different possibilities. She experienced people of different races, religions, and ideas. She saw the devastating effects of segregation in the southern states. Aretha was able to understand firsthand the importance of civil rights for all human beings.

A Surprising Situation

Back in Detroit and fifteen years old, Aretha found herself faced with a difficult situation. She was pregnant. Aretha has never publicly identified who the father of the baby is. Though the conservative Baptist Church might not have been accepting of her condition, Reverend Franklin stood by his daughter. He impressed upon her that she would be responsible for a new life, but he also continued to support her dreams of performing.

Several months after giving birth to her son Clarence (named after her father), Aretha rejoined her father's touring revue. Reverend Franklin wanted to continue preparing Aretha for a professional career. Big Mama and Erma took care of young Clarence back in Detroit.

A New Focus

At seventeen years old, Aretha was juggling teenage motherhood, high school, and a part-time

Despite growing up very quickly, young Aretha Franklin remained firm in her search for success as a singer.

career as a gospel performer. The Franklins had moved to a larger home in a wealthy section of Detroit. Aretha managed to find time for love as well. She began dating a man a few years older than herself. They met at a local roller-skating rink. Aretha fell in love, but soon learned that her boyfriend was cheating on her. Unfortunately, before she got wise, she got pregnant again.

Aretha's father reacted with the same compassion he had shown during her first pregnancy. He continued to believe that a great career lay ahead for Aretha. Aretha gave birth to her second son, Eddie. She decided that she needed to focus on motherhood and on her own singing career. After careful consideration, Aretha dropped out of high school. With Big Mama's help raising her two sons, Aretha began to take steps toward a professional career.

1942
Aretha Louise Franklin is born in Memphis, Tennessee, on March 25.

1966
Aretha switches record labels and signs with Atlantic Records.

1968
Aretha wins another Grammy Award for "Chain of Fools." She also performs at the funeral of Dr. Martin Luther King Jr.

1960
Aretha, at age eighteen, signs a recording contract with Columbia Records.

1967
"Respect" wins Aretha her first Grammy Awards for Best Rhythm and Blues Recording and Best R & B Solo Vocal Performance, Female.

1972
Aretha sings at the funeral of family friend, gospel singer Mahalia Jackson. Aretha returns to her gospel roots by recording *Amazing Grace*. The double album becomes the biggest selling gospel recording in history.

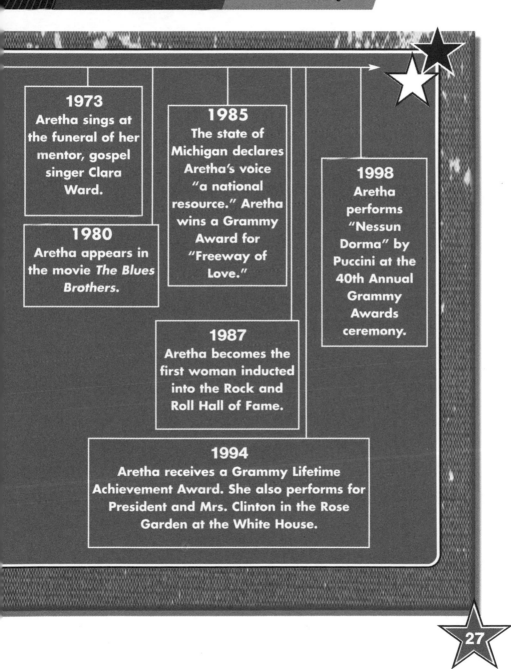

1973
Aretha sings at the funeral of her mentor, gospel singer Clara Ward.

1980
Aretha appears in the movie *The Blues Brothers.*

1985
The state of Michigan declares Aretha's voice "a national resource." Aretha wins a Grammy Award for "Freeway of Love."

1987
Aretha becomes the first woman inducted into the Rock and Roll Hall of Fame.

1998
Aretha performs "Nessun Dorma" by Puccini at the 40th Annual Grammy Awards ceremony.

1994
Aretha receives a Grammy Lifetime Achievement Award. She also performs for President and Mrs. Clinton in the Rose Garden at the White House.

The First Recordings

Reverend Franklin's tours were very successful. Thousands of people bought tickets for his performances. Aretha, like all of the performers in the revue, was paid a salary for her work. Though she was still known as "Reverend Franklin's daughter," Aretha was also gaining fans of her own.

Aretha's First Album

Before her sons were born, Aretha had recorded some

gospel music on the Chess Records label. That first album combined material recorded at New Bethel Baptist Church in Detroit with recordings Aretha made on the road in her father's show. The album included "Precious Lord," "The Day Is Past and Gone" (made famous by Clara Ward), and "Never Grow Old."

Aretha was approached to record with a local Detroit label, Motown Records. Today, Motown is famous for an incredible lineup of stars: the Supremes, the Temptations, Stevie Wonder, and Gladys Knight and the Pips. In 1960, however, the label was not well known. Despite their admiration for Berry Gordy Jr., the founder of Motown, Reverend Franklin and Aretha decided to hold out for an offer from a more established company. They decided to send Aretha to New York City, where most of the major music labels had headquarters.

New York

Reverend Franklin had connections in New York City who could help Aretha find a recording

John Hammond, pictured here circa 1945, signed eighteen-year-old Aretha to Columbia Records.

contract. One of those connections was bass player Major Holley. Holley agreed to help Aretha record a demo record. The demo included the songs "My Funny Valentine" and "Today I Sing the Blues." Aretha's chaperone in New York was a woman named Jo King, who later became Aretha's first manager. Jo delivered Aretha's demo to John Hammond at Columbia Records.

John Hammond was a white record producer at Columbia who loved African American music. He signed the famous jazz singer Billie Holiday to her Columbia recording contract during the 1930s. John was very impressed with Aretha's demo, particularly "Today I Sing the Blues." Aretha's recording of the song showcased her range and mature, soulful voice. It was hard for John to believe that the vocalist he was hearing was only eighteen years old! John arranged to meet Aretha, and he immediately signed her to a six-year recording contract with Columbia Records.

Recording *Aretha*

Aretha and John respected each other from the beginning. He was impressed with her maturity, and she trusted his judgment in selecting material for her first album. John arranged for Aretha to record her first album using musicians he had chosen. Playing piano was Ray Bryant, an up-and-coming jazz musician who also came from a gospel background. On bass was Bill Lee, the father of filmmaker Spike Lee. The group also included musicians from Duke Ellington's orchestra.

The album *Aretha* was an unusual mix of songs. The first single released was "Today I Sing the Blues." The album also included the Judy

The Attraction of Secular Music

Aretha's album with Chess Records showcased her gospel talent, but she wanted to perform other styles of music, too. With her father's blessing, Aretha decided to sing secular music as well as gospel. "Secular" refers to music that is not church music. Gospel music is focused on spiritual themes; secular music addresses more down-to-earth issues like love and sexuality.

During Aretha's childhood, many gospel singers began attempting professional careers that included jazz, blues, R & B, and pop material. Dinah Washington (born Ruth Lee Jones) was a young gospel singer and pianist. In 1943, when she was nineteen years old, Dinah began singing jazz songs in Chicago nightclubs where she was discovered by bandleader Lionel Hampton. Dinah's career took off, and she became a well-known jazz and pop singer.

Sam Cooke was also a successful gospel performer who crossed over to the world of pop and R & B. He took the performance techniques that he used as a gospel singer and applied them to his career as a pop singer. Sam Cooke wrote or cowrote many of his secular hits, including "You Send Me."

Unfortunately, there was some backlash to the success of these gospel crossovers. Many churchgoing African Americans felt that gospel singers should not pursue careers in secular music. But Aretha was fortunate. Her father allowed her to pursue her musical talents in any style she wanted to explore. Aretha's first album on the Columbia Records label showcased her ability to sing songs of any style. Her first successful single was a blues song, "Today I Sing the Blues."

Garland tune "Somewhere Over the Rainbow," and "It Ain't Necessarily So" from the opera *Porgy and Bess*. "Today I Sing the Blues" was successful on the R & B charts (also known as the race charts because they tracked nonwhite listeners), but *Aretha* did not have any major hits.

Working Professionally

Aretha was now a professional recording artist, but she still had a lot to learn. Aretha's manager Jo King arranged for her to take "finishing classes" in preparation for live performances. Aretha took classes in posture and movement. She had a vocal coach. Her favorite classes were dancing lessons with Cholly Atkins, a famous black choreographer. Cholly later went on to work with Motown acts like Diana Ross and the Supremes.

Aretha also began performing live concerts at small clubs in New York City's Greenwich Village. Initially, Aretha suffered from terrible stage fright at the New York clubs. Sometimes she didn't show up as scheduled. When she did show up, audiences loved her. It was clear to everyone that Aretha had an incredible voice. The album *Aretha* was so successful that she was named the New Female Vocal Star in the 1961 International Jazz Critics Poll.

Aretha's nerves got the best of her when she was booked to appear as a guest on *The Ed Sullivan Show*. The show was a great opportunity for a young artist, since Ed Sullivan drew large audiences. Aretha wore a gown that had been made especially for the appearance, but network censors told her she would have to wear

Fun Fact!

Aretha Franklin was the first woman to be inducted into the Rock and Roll Hall of Fame, in 1987. She also broke new ground when she graced the cover of *Time* magazine in 1968. Aretha was the first female African American to appear on its cover.

something else. "They said my gown was too low cut, [but] I don't think it was," Aretha remembered years later. "I don't think that at that time they had seen a black woman on network TV showing so much cleavage. I had rehearsed a long time for that appearance. I just went out the back door crying."

Aretha continued touring and performing in other cities. At a concert in Philadelphia, Clara Ward and the Ward Singers went to see Aretha perform. John Wilson, a pianist for the Wards, recalled that Aretha was terribly nervous. "Aretha sang wonderfully for an empty house, but she was pleased to see Clara," Wilson explained. "Aretha was feeling low but Clara encouraged her to continue." Aretha took Clara Ward's advice and kept on trying.

A New Romance

On one of her visits to Detroit, Aretha met an old friend of Dinah Washington's, Ted White. Aretha had met Ted in her childhood, when he and Dinah had visited the Franklin house. Though he was eleven years older than she was,

Ted and Aretha shared a birthday, March 25. Aretha was immediately attracted to him.

Ted had a reputation for being a ladies' man. He took Aretha out on the town though she knew he was dating other women. Reverend Franklin was not pleased. He had high expectations of his daughters, and wanted to see them marry men he thought were responsible and loving. Ted White didn't meet with Reverend Franklin's approval. Though it made her father angry, Aretha continued to see Ted White.

In 1961, Aretha married Ted. To everyone's surprise, she did not have a big wedding in her father's church. Instead, they were married on the road between performances. Almost immediately, Ted White took over management of Aretha's career. Later that year, she gave birth to her third son, Ted Jr.

Try, Try Again

During Aretha's six years at Columbia Records, she recorded albums of jazz, blues, and pop material. She sang show tunes and ballads, traditional songs and new compositions.

Johnny Mathis enjoyed more success with white audiences than Aretha did due to his pop vocals.

Critics responded positively to Aretha's talent, but nothing seemed to catch the attention of radio listeners. The music industry was still segregated, with separate charts for black and white recording artists. The most successful black artist at Columbia was Johnny Mathis, who was being marketed exclusively to the white pop charts. Johnny Mathis didn't perform any songs that could be perceived as R & B or race music. Most radio listeners who loved his smooth vocals had no idea that he was African American.

Aretha sometimes had to sing songs that were arranged to appeal to white audiences, in the style of the Johnny Mathis hits. This often required the use of backup singers who sang in a very fixed and smooth manner. These songs also used heavy violins and other string instruments instead of the more soulful piano and bass arrangements. While Aretha still sang the lead vocal on these songs, the end result did not show what Aretha was capable of. None of them were hits.

Though Aretha recorded many albums, Columbia was sending confusing signals to record buyers. Since her voice was produced in many different ways, singing songs of many different styles, it was hard to identify Aretha's signature sound. Listeners weren't sure if Aretha Franklin was a jazz singer, a blues singer, or a pop crossover sensation!

In other ways, Columbia was the perfect training ground for Aretha. Thanks to John Hammond, she had access to the most professional musicians and record producers available. One of Aretha's favorite producers was Bob Mersey, who helped her arrange an album-length tribute to Dinah Washington shortly after Dinah's death in 1963. Bob Mersey was able

As time went on, Aretha found great success as both a recording artist and live performer.

to provide musical arrangements that highlighted Aretha's unique voice whether she was singing a noisy blues number or a heartbreaking ballad. The Dinah Washington tribute album, called *Unforgettable: A Tribute to Dinah Washington*, was one of Aretha's most successful albums at Columbia.

Aretha continued a heavy schedule of live performances. Her tours were getting longer and longer, and she was beginning to open for more successful artists, like Sam Cooke and Jackie Wilson. Touring with more professional artists, Aretha was learning about all elements of performing. The frightened young woman was slowly becoming more confident, and she was learning how to connect with her audiences.

Success at Atlantic

3

Though she had no major hit songs, Aretha's six years with Columbia Records had established her reputation as a talented singer. When other record labels heard that her six-year Columbia contract was nearing its end, she began getting offers. Aretha was most interested in Atlantic Records. Atlantic was a much smaller company than Columbia, but Aretha knew that might help her in the end.

Atlantic's Offer

Jerry Wexler was the Atlantic producer who approached Ted White about signing Aretha to his label. Jerry Wexler, like John Hammond at Columbia, was a producer who appreciated the talent of African American performers. At Atlantic, Wexler helped develop the careers of Ray Charles and Ruth Brown, two of the most successful black singers of the time. Wexler felt certain that he could help Aretha find greater success, too. With a $30,000 bonus for signing with Atlantic, Aretha happily agreed to switch labels in 1966.

Wexler was aware that Aretha had tremendous talent as a pianist and admired her gospel roots. He wanted Aretha to accompany herself on piano while she sang. Aretha was encouraged by these changes. She felt reassured by Wexler's involvement, but she was glad that he wanted her to be included in most of the production decisions. It was a very different experience than she had had at Columbia, where executives decided most of the details without asking for her input.

Jerry Wexler *(right)* of Atlantic Records enlisted white country and soul musicians at the Muscle Shoals studio for Aretha's first album on his label.

Down to Alabama

Jerry Wexler had very different ideas about the musicians who should perform with Aretha. Wexler frequently worked with a recording studio in Muscle Shoals, Alabama. In Muscle Shoals, Wexler had developed relationships with many white musicians who came from a unique background of country music and blues. The skill of these musicians added greatly to the recordings of Atlantic's African American artists. For Aretha's first Atlantic album, Jerry Wexler took her to Muscle Shoals in January 1967.

In Alabama, Aretha clicked immediately with the white studio musicians. They were all professionals and were able to understand what Aretha had in mind for her first song, "I Never Loved a Man (the Way I Love You)." Aretha played acoustic piano in the recording sessions.

Aretha's first day of recording in Alabama was remarkable. "Everybody stopped in their tracks," when they heard Aretha sing, remembered one of the engineers. The other musicians were inspired by Aretha's earthy, bluesy delivery of the first song. "I Never Loved a Man (the Way I Love You)" was about a woman who couldn't bring herself to leave a man even though he abused her. That song was finished during the first day of recording, and that same day they began work on a second track, "Do Right Woman, Do Right Man."

Following the first day's recordings, Aretha and Ted White spent the night at a nearby motel with the other musicians. White had been drinking during the day, and he began to argue with one of the white musicians. Producer Jerry Wexler was awakened by the noise of the argument, which soon became more violent. After the fight, a drunken Ted blamed Jerry for bringing Aretha to work with "rednecks." By morning, Aretha and Ted were gone. Aretha's new album was incomplete.

A Tough Marriage

Ted White was not an easy man to get along with. There were many occasions when he lost his temper. He argued with Aretha, producers, and musicians. He drank heavily, which only made his fights worse. "Drinking finally destroyed our relationship," Aretha would admit many years later.

Aretha stuck with Ted for a long time, despite his violent temper and his drinking problems. When they married, Aretha was still a shy young woman of nineteen. By the time she signed with Atlantic, though, Aretha was twenty-four. She was becoming more comfortable with herself and with her future as a professional musician. She began to rely more on herself and less on the men around her, including Ted.

Throughout 1967 and 1968 Aretha's success was astounding. At the same time, her marriage to Ted became increasingly difficult. Aretha would triumph over her difficult marriage, but not without paying a price. During a time in which she deserved to focus on her tremendous success, Aretha was often forced to waste time and energy fighting with her husband. Though she was soon to become a world-famous star, Aretha's life was not so different from the lives of other emotionally abused women.

The First Hits

Jerry Wexler's instincts about Aretha were on target. When he returned to New York after the one-day recording session in Muscle Shoals, Jerry knew he had a hit single on his hands. He began to distribute copies of "I Never Loved a Man (the Way I Love You)" to radio disc jockeys. The song was an instant radio sensation.

Aretha's sisters Carolyn and Erma flew to New York to help her finish recording "Do Right Woman, Do Right Man." By overdubbing (layering one sound track over another), Aretha was able to play both the piano part and the organ part for the song. Combined with the vocal power of the three Franklin sisters, the track was another hit. "Do Right Woman, Do Right Man" was released as the B-side of "I Never Loved a Man (the Way I Love You)."

The single sold 250,000 copies in its first two weeks of release. Only weeks later it would become Aretha's first million-selling single. The song hit the top ten of the pop charts, and rode at the top of the R & B charts at the same time.

Aretha had more hits ready to be recorded. She reworked "Respect," a song written by singer Otis Redding. Otis Redding was another Atlantic artist produced by Jerry Wexler, and he was one of Atlantic's most successful stars, making a big impression with his brand of soul music.

Jerry Wexler and Aretha display two of her gold records.

Off and Running

Aretha's first album on the Atlantic label, *I Never Loved a Man the Way I Love You*, was released in March 1967. Partly due to the success of the song "I Never Loved a Man (the Way I Love You)," the album was a big hit. The next big single to hit the charts was "Respect." With its driving

From Rhythm and Blues to Soul

Rhythm and blues (R & B) developed during the post–World War II years in America. The "rhythm" came from drumbeats and the electric bass and guitar lines that were the backbone of so many danceable tunes in the 1940s and 1950s. The "blues" of R & B incorporated the vocal traditions of southern blues songs and included gospel traditions as well. In the 1950s, teenagers, in particular, began listening to R & B, which provided them with music they could dance to. Individual performers began to make their mark with louder, jumpier tunes, including Chuck Berry ("Johnny B. Goode") and Little Richard ("Tutti Frutti").

Soul music was R & B music of the late 1960s and early 1970s. It was a time of growing pride for many African Americans, as major strides were made during the civil rights movement. Soul music gave voice to that pride and, as with Aretha's music, addressed hard-hitting issues of love, respect, sex, and freedom.

Soul music had different categories. Chicago soul was rooted in gospel, like the work of Aretha and Sam Cooke and vocal groups like the Supremes and the Temptations. Southern soul made stars of Ray Charles and James Brown, combining traditional blues with string orchestras and other unusual arrangements. There were even a few white soul artists, like the British singer Dusty Springfield.

Soul music continued to evolve: funk and fusion music grew from soul, and later hip-hop and even rap found inspiration from the same sources.

energy and catchy backup vocals, the song became Aretha's signature number. It also won her two Grammy Awards, for Best Rhythm & Blues Recording and Best R & B Solo Vocal Performance, Female.

Aretha herself wrote "Dr. Feelgood," which was another smash hit. The racy song told the humorous story of a woman who just wants to stay home with her man. Aretha's delivery of the song was very sexy, and it allowed her to vocalize in a way

Fun Fact!

The Queen of Soul's first name has appeared in many of her album titles. She recorded two albums called *Aretha*. The first one was released in 1961, the other in 1986. She has also released albums titled *Aretha Arrives*, *Aretha Now*, *Aretha in Paris*, and *Aretha After Hours*, to name a few.

she'd never done on any of her material at
Columbia Records.

Aretha quickly became recognized for the
honest and emotional delivery of her songs. This
honesty was particularly appealing in "Respect"
and "Dr. Feelgood" because they featured Aretha
as an independent woman, demanding
satisfaction from her life and her partners.
"Respect" and other songs also featured call-and-
response style vocals with her backup singers,
very much in the gospel singing tradition.

More Hits

Without taking a break, Aretha went into the
studio to record a second album for Atlantic
that was released in August 1967, only four
months after the release of the first album.
Aretha Arrives included yet another big hit,
"Baby, I Love You." In addition to recording the
new album, Aretha began touring to support
her hit songs.

Though she had spent a lot of time on the
road during her years at Columbia, nothing

By the age of twenty-five, Aretha's first two albums on Atlantic Records had rocketed her to superstardom.

could have prepared her for the instant success of her first two Atlantic albums. Aretha's live concerts were in demand across the country, and she eagerly made the appearances expected of her. The work was exhausting, but Aretha tried to schedule her tours to allow time for her voice and body to rest. It was an exciting time for twenty-five-year-old Aretha, who was now a genuine singing superstar.

4

Voice of Her Time

By early 1968 there was no doubt that Aretha was a complete success. She had a string of hit records to her credit in just one year's time. Huge crowds paid to see her perform live wherever she traveled. Her success spread far beyond the R & B charts of the United States. Aretha's appearances sold out in Europe and South America as well as New York City, Los Angeles, and Las Vegas.

Getting Some Respect

Aretha's songs, voice, and style came along at the right time. "Respect" in particular hit a chord with the American public. "Respect" echoed the feelings of thousands of people throughout 1967, which was a year of struggle and change. Aretha sang the song from a woman's point of view, laying it on the line for her man and telling him what she expected from him. The song had a universal appeal, though, and people of all races, genders, and ages could understand the desire for respect and equal treatment. The song became an anthem for people struggling in the civil rights and women's rights movements.

Like her father, Aretha was "color-blind" in her professional relationships. She worked easily with white producers and musicians and considered many of them personal friends. Her success in working with people of all colors gave Aretha a unique perspective on the civil rights struggle. Her life was proof that an African American woman could be financially

Aretha shakes hands with audience members at the Soul Together concert that took place at Madison Square Garden in September 1968.

successful and gain the respect of men and women of any color.

A Time for Change

Aretha's involvement with civil rights went back to her days as Reverend Franklin's daughter. Just as Reverend Franklin had exposed her to artists of many different kinds, he had also introduced her to people like Dr. Martin Luther King Jr. Reverend Franklin supported Dr. King's philosophy of nonviolent protest against discrimination. The two men often made public appearances together. They were both preachers in the Baptist Church.

It was difficult for Aretha to speak out publicly for political causes once her career was in full swing. Singers were expected to entertain people, not voice their political opinions. Aretha supported Dr. King in any way she could. She often performed concerts that benefited the Southern Christian Leadership Council (SCLC), the organization that pursued Dr. King's objectives of equal rights for all people. If Reverend Franklin asked Aretha to support similar causes, she could be counted on to be there and do whatever she could. There were occasions when Aretha's political positions were made crystal clear. Though she was proud to perform for mixed-race audiences, or for people of color, there were occasions in the South where she was asked to perform before white-only audiences. Even after the passage of civil rights legislation during the 1960s, many areas of the American South remained segregated. Aretha refused to perform at any venue that was segregated.

Did You Know?

Aretha has recorded duets with Whitney Houston, Annie Lennox, George Michael, and Elton John. Her willingness to work with people in other genres of music has brought her much success. Each of her duets with these artists has made it onto the charts!

Aretha accepts her third Grammy Award, for "Chain of Fools," which earned her the prize for Best R & B Performance, Female.

The Queen of Soul

Aretha's album *Lady Soul* was released in January 1968. Aretha played keyboards and got support from many of the musicians from Muscle Shoals. Aretha and Ted White cowrote "Since You've Been Gone (Sweet Sweet Baby)," which went to number five on the pop charts (it reached number one on the R & B charts). Even more successful was "Chain of Fools," which went to number two on the pop charts. "Chain of Fools" won Aretha her third Grammy, for Best R & B Performance, Female.

Lady Soul also contained songs written by soul musicians James Brown and Curtis Mayfield. Aretha's sister Carolyn wrote the beautiful gospel number "Ain't No Way." The song featured Whitney Houston's mother, Cissy, on backup. Even guitarist Eric Clapton (of the British groups Cream and the Yardbirds) was featured on "Good to Me as I Am to You."

Perhaps most remarkable was "(You Make Me Feel Like) A Natural Woman." Like "Respect," "A Natural Woman" became one of her signature numbers. Carole King, who wrote "A Natural

Woman," also had great success singing the song on her own 1970 album, *Tapestry.*

As she had in 1967, Aretha recorded a second album within the same year. *Aretha Now* included her cover of the Dionne Warwick hit "I Say a Little Prayer." Aretha's version quickly hit the top ten on the pop charts. "Think," "See Saw," and Aretha's cover of Sam Cooke's "You Send Me" were other hits from the album. It seemed Aretha's string of hit songs would never stop.

Feeling the Love

As her career with Atlantic was beginning, a radio DJ in Chicago gave Aretha the title Queen of Soul. Aretha appeared at a ceremony and smiled as the audience roared their approval. She was even given a real crown to wear at the event!

By February 1968, Aretha's Detroit fans wanted to celebrate the success of their hometown girl. The mayor of Detroit announced February 16 as "Aretha Franklin Day." The publishers of various music magazines, including *Record World* and *Billboard,* awarded her the title of Female Vocalist of the Year. Dr. Martin Luther King Jr. flew in as a surprise guest to present her with a special award from the SCLC for her charitable work. It was a moment of triumph and achievement for Aretha.

The Assassination of MLK

Two months after presenting Aretha with her award, Dr. King was assassinated in Memphis, Tennessee. King had been visiting Memphis to support garbage workers in a nonviolent strike. He was shot to death outside his motel room.

King's death was a terrible blow to many Americans of all colors. As his personal friends, it was especially hard for the Franklin family. At King's funeral in Atlanta, both Aretha and gospel great Mahalia Jackson performed. Aretha sang King's favorite hymn, "Precious Lord, Take My Hand."

Aretha continued performing during the next several months, bringing audiences together in their grief. In June, Aretha sang at a benefit produced by Jerry Wexler to support the

Civil Rights

The civil rights movement in the United States was a reaction to discrimination that prevented African Americans from enjoying the same quality of life as white people. Though slavery was abolished in the 1860s, segregation prevented African Americans from using many public facilities, and they were frequently denied the rights that whites enjoyed, including the right to vote.

Though African American music broke many barriers, the black artists who performed the music continued to face severe discrimination during the first half of the twentieth century. Black performers were often denied the right to eat at or even enter through the front door of the establishments where they performed. Many white-owned radio stations refused to play "race music," just as many white record labels refused to record or distribute black artists. The experience of these musicians mirrored the everyday lives of black Americans who faced discrimination at every level imaginable.

Dr. Martin Luther King Jr. organized many nonviolent protests through his Southern Christian Leadership Council. In March 1963, King organized the March on Washington, D.C., in which more than 200,000 supporters of civil rights marched to the Lincoln Memorial. The actions of these protesters paved the way for the successful passage of the Civil Rights Act of 1964, which prohibited discrimination in education and employment. It was a major victory for the movement.

Martin Luther King Jr. Fund. The benefit took place at Madison Square Garden in New York City. More than 20,000 people attended the concert.

An Uncomfortable Spotlight

In late June 1968, Aretha was featured on the cover of *Time* magazine, which was doing a story on the success of soul music. Aretha was thrilled to be included in such a major magazine, but the results of the interview were not what she expected. The *Time* article focused on some extremely personal areas of Aretha's life. It referred to her struggles with weight and smoking and her marriage to Ted White, suggesting that he was physically abusive. The article also linked Aretha's life directly to the lyrics of the songs she sang, especially the sadder blues numbers.

Aretha felt the article was unfair. She was angry that it included quotes from Mahalia Jackson and her own brother, Cecil Franklin, that she felt were untrue. Even as a major star, Aretha didn't feel she had a fair chance to tell her side of the story. In reaction to the *Time* article, Aretha didn't give interviews for several years.

End of the Road

Despite the difficulties she encountered in 1968, Aretha maintained her busy touring schedule. She recorded a live album in Paris, France. She toured Germany, Holland, Sweden, Italy, and the Netherlands. She broke her leg in Hawaii, but performed a concert there in a wheelchair. She performed the national anthem at the 1968 Democratic Convention in Chicago.

In her personal life, Aretha had reached the end of her marriage to Ted White. Worn down by his drinking and abuse, Aretha divorced Ted in late 1968. It was a relief for some of Aretha's friends and family, who feared that Ted was not treating her well. For Aretha it was the end of a turbulent time with a man she had loved.

5

Down but Never Out

Following her divorce from Ted White, Aretha's life hit some bumps. There were reports of reckless driving, disorderly behavior, and too much drinking. She slowed down her hectic concert schedule. She spent less time in the recording studio. On the heels of the *Time* magazine article, some people wondered what was up with Aretha.

Taking a Break

Aretha had good reason to take a break. The year 1968 had been an intense one full of extreme highs and lows. There were many things to be proud of, including her successful European tour. Still, Aretha needed time to relax, think, and spend time with her three children in Detroit. Big Mama was still caring for Clarence and Eddie. Ted White and his own mother were raising Teddy Jr. Aretha took her time before recording or touring again.

In 1969, Atlantic released two new Aretha albums, both of them recorded in previous years. One of them, *Soul '69*, was actually an album of pop standards with a big band orchestra backing Aretha's vocals. The other album, *Aretha's Gold*, combined previous hits from 1967 and 1968 with a new song, "The House That Jack Built." Aretha had no major radio hits in 1969, but she was still getting plenty of airplay. Her fans loved the new albums and were eager to see Aretha tour again.

It wasn't all smooth sailing, though. At Aretha's Detroit home in December 1969, a drunken Ted White shot one of Aretha's houseguests. The guest did not die, but the experience frightened Aretha. A few months later, Ted again burst into Aretha's home in

Aretha with her fourth son, Kecalf, whose father is Ken "Wolf" Cunningham, her former road manager

Detroit and caused a scene. Aretha's father was involved in the argument, and Aretha broke down. She was unable to perform the following night at a sold-out concert in Chicago. She was dazed when she performed in St. Louis a few days later, and members of the audience demanded their money back.

Love Again

When Aretha did decide to go back to the studio in 1969, she recorded the album *This Girl's in Love with You.* Aretha won a fourth Grammy for the song "Share Your Love with Me." The album also included a love song she wrote, "Call Me," which did very well on the charts. The song was based on her own recent experiences. She was falling in love again.

In the fall of 1969, Aretha again toured Europe. Her road manager on the tour was a successful businessman named Ken Cunningham (Aretha called him Wolf). Aretha and Ken worked well together, and their professional relationship became an important friendship in her life. Gradually, that friendship blossomed into a romance.

It had been close to a year since Aretha's divorce, and Ken was going through a divorce of his own. Ken had a deep respect for Aretha as both an artist and a human being. Aretha's romance with Ken was very different from her marriage to Ted White. She and Ken began living together in New York City. In 1970, she gave birth to their son, Kecalf (pronounced "Kelf"). Kecalf's name was an acronym spelled from the initials of his father (K-E-C) and mother (A-L-F).

Spirit of Success

Aretha's career got back on track in 1970. She released the album *Spirit in the Dark*, which got great reviews. The title track was a gospel-style number with a rock beat. "Don't Play That Song" was the biggest hit, and it garnered Aretha yet another Grammy Award.

Aretha's live performances received even greater reviews. In Spain, she performed at a bullfighting arena for 40,000 people. She appeared at the Apollo Theater in Harlem and "sang soulfully—she sighed, screamed, hollered, and sang," according to the *New York Times*. The power of Aretha's live performances thrilled her old fans and made new fans of unlikely people. Some of the unlikeliest fans were the hippies of San Francisco.

In 1971, Jerry Wexler arranged for Aretha to perform a concert at the Fillmore West, an auditorium that was famous for presenting hard-edged bands like the Grateful Dead. No one in Aretha's team knew what to expect from a San Francisco audience. There was no need to worry—the flower children loved Aretha! Aretha was comfortable in the crowded room, performing with a band of great soul musicians brought together especially for the event. She brought surprise guest Ray Charles onstage to perform "Spirit in the Dark" with her. Their duet brought the house down. Atlantic's recording of the concert became one of Aretha's most successful albums.

Amazing Grace

In January 1972, Aretha recorded her first gospel album since becoming a major star. Jerry Wexler supported her idea completely. After the success of her live concert and the album recorded there at the Fillmore West, Atlantic was eager to have another live Aretha concert on record. Wexler arranged for Aretha to perform at the New Temple Missionary Baptist Church in Los Angeles.

Aretha was excited and nervous. There was still a lot of resistance to gospel singers who crossed over to sing pop, jazz, and R & B. After hearing Aretha sing at Mahalia Jackson's funeral, the gospel singer Sallie Martin said, "Worst thing I ever heard—a nightclub singer at a gospel singer's funeral." Martin was not alone in her opinion. There were many African Americans who felt Aretha had no right to go back to singing gospel.

Aretha's musical support came from Reverend James Cleveland, his church choir and several musicians from Atlantic Records. The results were electric. The album, *Amazing Grace*, captured the energy of a live gospel performance. Throughout the recording the audience reacted with applause and singing, and they shouted "Amen!"

Aretha's father, Reverend Franklin, got up to speak to the congregation. "I was just about to bust wide open," he said. "You talk about being moved. Not only because Aretha is my daughter, Aretha is just a stone singer . . . if you want to know the truth, she has never left the church." *Amazing Grace*, the double album of Aretha's return to her musical roots, became the best-selling gospel album of all time!

Aretha holds up her Grammy for Best R & B Female Performer, which she won in 1972.

Good-bye to Old Friends

In 1972, the great gospel singer Mahalia Jackson died. Aretha performed at Jackson's funeral in Chicago, singing "Precious Lord, Take My Hand" as she had at Dr. King's funeral. It was a great loss for Aretha, who had looked up to Jackson since childhood.

One year later, Aretha's mentor and inspiration, Clara Ward, passed away. Aretha later remembered Clara as "dramatic, daring, exciting, [and] courageous." Ward always encouraged Aretha to perform, and she inspired much of Aretha's personal performance style. It was a great loss. At Ward's funeral, Aretha sang "The Day Is Past and Gone," in honor of her old friend.

A Comfortable Groove

The year 1972 was a good one for Aretha. Early in the year she released an album, *Young, Gifted, and Black*. The album included still more hits, like "Rock Steady" and a cover of Otis Redding's "I've Been Loving You Too Long." She won Grammys for "Rock Steady" and for her

79

gospel album *Amazing Grace.* She was very much in love with Ken Cunningham. At public appearances, it was obvious that Aretha had lost a lot of weight and was living a healthier lifestyle.

Aretha felt comfortable enough to be interviewed again, too. In an interview with *Ebony* magazine, she said, "Anybody who has kept up with my career knows that I've had my share of problems and trouble, but look at me today. I'm here, I have my health, I'm strong, I have my career and my family and plenty of friends everywhere." It was clearly a happy time for Aretha.

During the mid '70s, radio listeners gradually lost interest in soul music. Their tastes moved on to funk and disco. Aretha and Jerry Wexler tried to incorporate these new sounds into her albums, but were not always successful. Though she continued to win Grammy Awards through 1974, her long winning streak finally stopped. In 1975, Natalie Cole won the Grammy for Best R & B Vocal Performance, Female. Natalie was the daughter of pop singer Nat "King" Cole, and she had grown up idolizing Aretha Franklin.

Despite slower album sales, Aretha continued to record some incredible songs. With the help of producer Curtis Mayfield, Aretha recorded an album of songs from the movie *Sparkle* in 1976. That album included a beautiful ballad, "Something He Can Feel," which was revived many years later by the group En Vogue.

Separate Ways

Though she had slimmed down during her years with Ken Cunningham, Aretha had not managed to quit smoking. She was still smoking up to two packs of cigarettes a day, which was terrible for her health and voice. Ken had often warned her that she would encounter health problems unless she managed to quit smoking. During a concert in Pittsburgh, Aretha found that she couldn't catch her breath. She knew she was headed for trouble. Unfortunately, there was more trouble in store.

Aretha's brother, Cecil, had been her business manager for several years and he began to have disagreements with Ken. There were no violent

81

By 1978, Aretha Franklin had split up with Ken Cunningham and married actor Glynn Turman.

arguments as there might have been with Ted White, but the friction between the two men made Aretha unhappy.

Aretha moved to Los Angeles during this time. Ken was happier living in New York and he kept his home there. Gradually they grew apart. They had shared a long, successful relationship, but in 1977 they broke up. Aretha was single again for the first time in many years. But not for long!

Wedding Bells

In Los Angeles, Aretha met actor Glynn Turman. Turman had been a successful stage actor who was now working in television and films. Aretha knew his work from the movie *Cooley High*. They began dating and soon fell in love. In late 1977, Glynn asked Aretha to marry him. She said yes.

At last Aretha was able to plan the big wedding she had always wanted in Detroit. Though her father was wary of Glynn because Aretha had not known him for very long, he agreed to marry them at New Bethel Baptist Church. On April 11, 1978, Aretha and Glynn were married. Prior to their wedding, they signed a prenuptial agreement that protected Aretha's finances and property in the event of a divorce.

The wedding was beautiful. Aretha's sister, Carolyn, and her cousin, Brenda, both performed songs they had written especially for the event. Aretha was surrounded by her large family and hundreds of friends. The following day, Aretha and Glynn hosted a reception in Beverly Hills for 500 people. Photographers from *Time* and *Ebony* captured the festivities.

New Possibilities

Aretha enjoyed her married life in Los Angeles. She and Glynn were living with her four sons and his three children from a previous marriage, so it was a busy household. With Glynn's encouragement she was also considering acting opportunities. Aretha accepted a part in the film *The Blues Brothers*, starring Dan Ackroyd and John Belushi. In the film, Aretha plays a waitress who tries to stop her man from joining a traveling blues band. She performed her song "Think" and received great reviews.

Jerry Wexler had resigned from Atlantic Records. Aretha's albums on Atlantic were not doing well. She feared that the company wasn't doing enough to promote her music. Aretha began considering other offers.

Tragedy Strikes Again

Prior to the 1980 release of *The Blues Brothers,* Aretha was busy preparing for a series of shows at the Aladdin Hotel in Las Vegas. On June 10, 1979, she came off stage at the end of a performance. Her husband and her brother were waiting for her. Cecil told her that their father had been shot in Detroit. Aretha was in shock.

As she made plans to return immediately to Detroit, Aretha tried to understand what had happened. During a robbery at her father's house, Reverend Franklin had been shot in the knee and the groin. Neighbors managed to get into the house and phone for an ambulance.

Aretha reclines with husband
Glynn Turman in January 1981.

Though radio stations were announcing that Reverend Franklin had died, the hospital was telling Aretha that he was alive. In fact, Aretha's father was still alive, but he had slipped into a coma.

Aretha's life would never be the same again. For the next five years, Reverend Franklin remained in a coma. Everything in Aretha's life focused on her father's health. She performed benefits to raise money for his care. Her sisters, Carolyn and Erma, changed their lives so they could be near him at all times. Aretha's own health suffered. Her smoking was at an all-time high, and she gained a great deal of weight.

Aretha spent so much time in Detroit that her marriage to Glynn began to suffer. In an awful coincidence, Glynn's uncle was shot and killed the week after Reverend Franklin was shot. Glynn's career began to take him away from Los Angeles and that added further strain to the marriage.

Farewell

On July 27, 1984, Reverend Franklin passed away. He never awoke from the coma after being shot. Thousands of people stood outside New Bethel Baptist Church during his funeral. Reverend Jesse Jackson, an old friend of the Franklins, spoke at the service. "C.L. Franklin was not just rare but unique. He was born in poverty, but poverty could not stop him. His flower did blossom."

Aretha's father had touched the lives of so many people in a positive way. Aretha's faith helped her through her grief. As she told *Ebony* magazine many years earlier, "I feel a real kinship with God, and that's what's helped me out of the problems I've faced."

6

New Directions

After careful consideration, Aretha changed record labels in 1980. She had good memories of her years with Atlantic, but she felt a new company would be able to help develop her sound in a way that would attract new listeners. Aretha signed with Arista Records, headed by Clive Davis. Davis had helped launch the careers of Barry Manilow and Melissa Manchester, and he had revived the career of Dionne Warwick.

Trying Something New

During her first years at Arista, Aretha worked with Arif Mardin, who had arranged some of her early work at Atlantic Records. She tried many musical styles, though her trademark soul vocals were still strong. Following the release of her first Arista album, she went to England to perform for Queen Elizabeth II, Prince Charles, and his fiancée, Lady Diana. Returning home, she performed in New York City in concerts that received great reviews. She went back into the studio and recorded a second album, *Love All the Hurt Away*. Though some of her singles were successful, Aretha's albums did not perform as well as she hoped.

Happily, she was earning Grammy nominations again. In 1981, she won a Grammy for the song "Hold on I'm Comin'." The Grammy Award restored Aretha's confidence, and she invited singer Luther Vandross to produce her next album, *Get It Right*. Aretha knew that Vandross had talent, and she was happy to get the perspective of a younger performer. The first single, "Jump to It," was a huge hit and went to number one on the R & B charts. Aretha's son Clarence wrote "Givin' In" for the album, and her son Teddy played guitar.

Moving On

As Aretha's recording career was getting back on track, she was busier than ever. Throughout her father's hospitalization, Aretha had maintained a busy concert schedule that raised money to pay for his care. By late 1982, her marriage to Glynn Turman fell apart, and they divorced. Aretha left Los Angeles and moved back to Detroit.

Detroit soon became more than just Aretha's home. It became the home of her recording studio as well. After a bad experience on a small twin-engine airplane, Aretha developed a terrible fear of flying. That fear restricted her life in some ways, but Aretha made the best of it. For tours and other engagements, she used a deluxe tour bus to travel.

Financial Woes

After Aretha's success in the movie *The Blues Brothers*, she was open to other acting possibilities. An exciting opportunity came when the producers of a Broadway musical about Mahalia Jackson approached Aretha to play the lead. Aretha was very interested and she signed a contract to begin work on the show in May 1984. *Sing, Mahalia, Sing* was scheduled to begin touring after opening in New York. When the time came to begin rehearsals in New York City, however, Aretha did not arrive.

Aretha claimed that her fear of flying made it impossible for her to get to New York in time. Though she tried to get there using a tour bus, she began the trip too late. In any event, Aretha was unable to participate in *Sing, Mahalia, Sing.* The producers sued her for breaking their contract, and a court in New York State agreed. Aretha was forced to pay more than $200,000 in production costs for a show that never happened!

This was the beginning of a series of financial problems. The Internal Revenue Service sued Aretha for unpaid taxes during her years with Atlantic Records. She sued Atlantic for not paying her adequate royalties on her recordings. In reaction to problems with New York State, Aretha canceled a series of sold-out Carnegie Hall performances. It was a difficult time for Aretha, who was distracted by her father's illness and death. Eventually most of the financial matters were settled without going to court.

Who's Zoomin' Who?

In 1985, Clive Davis arranged for Aretha to work with a talented new producer, Narada Michael Walden, who produced songs on Whitney Houston's debut album. Aretha was impressed with Narada, who brought in excellent musicians such as saxophonist Clarence Clemons and guitar legend Carlos Santana. The album title, *Who's Zoomin' Who?* was a saying Aretha used when she was flirting with a man.

On *Who's Zoomin' Who?*,
Aretha performed a duet with
Annie Lennox of Eurythmics.

The album was a smash hit, featuring the
Grammy-winning song "Freeway of Love." That
song also became Aretha's very first music video.
In the video, Aretha got to drive a pink Cadillac.
She even sported a short, spiky punk hairdo!
The album also contained a powerful duet with
Annie Lennox from Eurythmics. The duet,
"Sisters Are Doin' It for Themselves," was a

song about empowered working women. Aretha's next album included the duet "I Knew You Were Waiting (for Me)" with George Michael, which won a Grammy Award in 1987.

Recognition and Grief

In 1987, Aretha received an incredible honor. She was the first woman to be inducted into the Rock and Roll Hall of Fame! "I have to say I never thought of myself as a rock 'n' roll singer," Aretha told the *New York Times*. "Mostly I'm just a singer. That spans the whole realm of music." Aretha's brother Cecil accepted the award on her behalf since Aretha was unable to attend the ceremony. Though she was pleased to be included in the Hall of Fame, she was needed at home. Carolyn Franklin had been diagnosed with terminal breast cancer.

Aretha and the entire Franklin family came together to support Carolyn as she battled cancer. Unfortunately, the disease was not detected until she was already quite ill, and she died on April 25, 1988. To add to the family's grief, Cecil

Franklin was diagnosed with lung cancer the following year, and he passed away in December 1989. These were terrible losses for Aretha's close-knit family.

Back on Top

In the late 1980s and early 1990s, Aretha's old Atlantic recordings were achieving popularity with a new generation. During the '80s Aretha rarely left Detroit, but following Cecil's death she began to travel more frequently. She was still frightened of flying, but she toured using a

Fun Fact!

Aretha's fear of flying in an airplane makes it hard for her to tour. Luckily, she is able to ride in a luxury tour bus from venue to venue. Aretha's tour bus includes a full kitchen, fax, phones, and a movie screen!

Aretha was one of many superstars who performed at President Bill Clinton's inauguration in January 1993.

special bus she had custom designed for maximum comfort.

In 1989, Aretha performed a concert at Radio City Music Hall in New York City. The *New York Post* said that Aretha's concert was wonderful and that she looked "trim, beautiful, and sexy." Critics loved her performance at Radio City and nearly all of them wrote about how wonderful her voice still was. Not long after, the awards really started pouring in.

In January 1993, Aretha performed at President Bill Clinton's January inauguration ceremony in Washington, D.C. In 1994, she was awarded a Grammy Lifetime Achievement Award. That same year, Aretha was asked to again sing for the president of the United States. Aretha performed in the Rose Garden at the White House, in front of the president and first lady, as well as the emperor and empress of Japan. Later that year, Aretha was one of five recipients of the Kennedy Center Honors, an award that is given to artists who make valuable contributions to American culture.

Still Breaking New Ground

Aretha hasn't stopped singing and she hasn't stopped trying new musical sounds and styles. When Arista released a greatest hits album in 1994, Aretha added two new tracks. One of the new tunes, "Willing to Forgive," was produced by Kenneth "Babyface" Edmonds. The other was

What Is a Diva?

In the world of opera, a prima donna (Italian for "first lady") is the most important female performer. Prima donnas are often seen as grand, dramatic women, and are sometimes accused of having enormous egos and demanding personalities. When the singing of the prima donna excites opera fans, they will applaud loudly at the end of her song (an aria) and shout "Diva!" "Diva" is the Latin word for goddess.

Over the years the word "diva" has been used to praise talented women, but it has also taken on some of the negative associations of prima donna behavior. Depending on the situation, calling a performer a diva may be a compliment of her talent and beauty. But it might also be an insult, suggesting that she is vain, self-centered, or too demanding.

As an incredibly talented singer and a powerful, self-confident African American woman, Aretha has been called a diva in both senses of the word. More often than not, Aretha is referred to as a diva because she generously shares her talent with others and reaches the highest levels of professionalism. At the 1998 Grammy Awards, Aretha got to translate her diva status, literally, into operatic terms!

Aretha was honored with a Lifetime Achievement Award that evening, and she sang "Respect" for the adoring audience. Opera star Luciano Pavarotti had been scheduled to sing later in the evening, performing his famous rendition of "Nessun Dorma," an aria from the opera *Turandot*. While Aretha was backstage, a producer announced that Pavarotti was not feeling well enough to perform. The producer asked Aretha if she could quickly fill in for Pavarotti by singing the aria.

The Queen of Soul, between two of the Backstreet Boys, during VH1's *Divas Live 2001, A Tribute to Aretha Franklin.*

"A Deeper Love," a cover of the dance hit by C&C Music Factory. "A Deeper Love" was an incredible dance hit for the fifty-two year old Aretha!

In 1998, she took even greater risks by working with some of hip hop's greatest producers, including Sean "Puffy" Combs. Lauryn Hill wrote and produced the track "A Rose Is Still A Rose." The song was another powerful women's anthem. Aretha told writer David Ritz, "Lauryn reminds me of myself in the studio, very kicked back. We clicked."

The Diva

Aretha has been recognized as a great diva on more than one occasion by the music video channel VH1. VH1 included Aretha in their *Divas Live* concert in 1998, alongside Celine Dion, Mariah Carey, Gloria Estefan, and Shania Twain. All of the performers were incredible that night, but Aretha brought the house down. She closed the concert with the gospel tune "Testimony."

Three years later, VH1 devoted the *Divas Live 2001* concert to Aretha. An unbelievable list of artists performed in honor of Aretha, including Marc Anthony, Nelly Furtado, Jill Scott, the Backstreet Boys, Janet Jackson, and Stevie Wonder. Aretha herself performed gospel tunes, as well as "Think" and "Chain of Fools." It was another incredible live performance from Aretha, now nearly sixty years old.

Aretha's incredible career continues. In late 2001, she scheduled tour dates in the Midwest and New England. She has plans to write a cookbook. Following the success of her operatic performance at the 1998 Grammys, she has toyed with the idea of recording an album of arias. There is no stopping Aretha Franklin. She's a great woman, a true diva, and a living legend!

SELECTED DISCOGRAPHY

1961 *Aretha*

1967 *Aretha Arrives*

1967 *I Never Loved a Man (the Way I Love You)*

1968 *Lady Soul*

1970 *Spirit in the Dark*

1970 *This Girl's in Love with You*

1971 *Live at the Fillmore West*

1971 *Young, Gifted, and Black*

1972 *Amazing Grace*

1981 *Love All the Hurt Away*

1985 *Who's Zoomin' Who?*

1992 *Queen of Soul*

1998 *A Rose Is Still a Rose*

GLOSSARY

acoustic Natural sound of a musical instrument with no electronic enhancement or modification.

anthem A song of praise or happiness, usually sacred in meaning.

audition A tryout; to perform in order to get a role.

bigotry The state of mind of someone whose beliefs are narrow-minded; intolerance of other beliefs.

charts A listing that ranks music sales; a way of calculating the popularity of music.

cover A performance of someone else's song.

diva An important, influential female performer.

induct To bring something in.

manager The person who helps an entertainer make performance choices.

pop Relating to popular music, as in "pop singer."

racist Someone who discriminates based on other people's ethnic backgrounds.

rehearse To practice for a performance or event.

rhythm and blues (R & B) Music including elements of blues and black folk music.

secular music A type of music that is not religious in nature, containing themes that are not related to religious groups.

segregation The separation of a race, class, or religious or ethnic group by discriminatory means.

soul Music that originated in black American gospel singing.

standard A famous song that is commonly known and sung.

tribute Giving credit to someone or something.

TO FIND OUT MORE

Arista Records
6 West 57th Street
New York, NY 10019
(212) 489-7400
Web site: http://www.arista.com

Rock and Roll Hall of Fame and Museum
One Key Plaza
Cleveland, OH 44114
(888) 764-ROCK (7625)
Web site: http://www.rockhall.com

Web Sites

Due to the changing nature of Internet links, the Rosen Publishing Group, Inc., has developed an online list of Web sites related to the subject of this book. This site is updated regularly. Please use this link to access the list:

http://www.rosenlinks.com/rrhf/afra/

FOR FURTHER READING

Bego, Mark. *Aretha Franklin: The Queen of Soul.* New York: Da Capo Press, Inc., 2001.

Heilbut, Tony. *The Gospel Sound: Good News and Bad Times.* New York: Proscenium Publishers, 1997.

Jones, Hettie. *Big Star Fallin' Mama: Five Women in Black Music.* New York: Viking Penguin, 1997.

McAvoy, Jim. *Aretha Franklin.* Broomall, PA: Chelsea House Publishers, 2001.

Sheafer, Silvia Anne. *Aretha Franklin: Motown Superstar.* Berkeley Heights, NJ: Enslow Publishers, 1996.

Works Cited

Franklin, Aretha. *From These Roots.* New York: Villard Books, 1999.

Gourse, Leslie. *Aretha Franklin: Lady Soul.* New York: Franklin Watts, 1995.

INDEX

A

Amazing Grace, 77, 80
"Amazing Grace" (song), 5
Aretha, 31–34, 35, 52
Aretha Arrives, 52, 53
Aretha Now, 52, 64
Aretha's Gold, 71
Arista Records, 88, 89, 97
Atlantic Records, 42–46, 47, 49,
        53–55, 71, 75, 76, 77, 85,
        88, 89, 92, 95

B

Big Mama (grandmother), 13,
        23, 25, 71
Blues Brothers, The, 84–85, 91
Brown, James, 51, 63

C

"Chain of Fools," 63, 103
Charles, Ray, 43, 51, 75
Chess Records, 29, 32
civil rights movement, 10, 22, 51,
        57–60, 61, 66–67
Columbia Records, 30–31, 33,
        37–40, 42, 43, 53, 55
Cooke, Sam, and the Soul
        Stirrers, 18, 20, 33, 41,
        51, 64
Cunningham, Kecalf (son), 74

Cunningham, Ken, 73–74, 80,
        81–83

D

Davis, Clive, 88, 92
"Deeper Love, A," 102
Divas Live (VH1), 102–103
"Do Right Woman, Do Right
        Man," 46, 48
"Dr. Feelgood," 52–53

E

Ebony magazine, 80, 84, 87
Ed Sullivan Show, The, 35–36

F

Franklin, Aretha
        and Arista Records, 88, 89, 97
        and Atlantic Records,
                42–46, 47, 53–55, 71, 75,
                76, 77, 85, 88, 89, 92, 95
        childhood of, 8–25
        children of, 23, 25, 37, 71,
                74, 84, 90
        and Columbia Records, 30–31,
                33, 37–40, 42, 43, 53, 55
        as diva, 99
        first album of, 28–29, 32
        Grammy Awards won, 7, 52,
                63, 73, 74, 79–80, 89, 93,
                94, 97, 99, 103

influences of, 6, 18–20

marriages/divorces, 37, 46, 69, 70, 74, 83–84, 87, 90

musical genres and, 6, 32, 37–40, 76–77, 89

personal problems of, 46–47, 68, 69, 70, 71–73, 80, 81–83, 85–87, 90, 91–92, 94–95

as Queen of Soul, 6, 11, 64

and racism, 22, 61

start in singing, 12, 17–21, 23–25

Franklin, Barbara Siggers (mother), 8, 10–11, 13

Franklin, Carolyn (sister), 8, 12, 48, 63, 84, 86, 94

Franklin, Cecil (brother), 8, 17, 68, 81–83, 85, 94–95

Franklin, Clarence (son), 23, 71, 90

Franklin, Clarence LaVaughn (father), 8, 9–10, 12, 13–17, 37, 57, 60, 73, 83–84, 90

and Aretha's singing career, 12, 17, 20, 23, 25, 29–30, 33, 77

and music tour, 20–22, 23, 28

shooting of, 85–86, 87

Franklin, Eddie (son), 25, 71

Franklin, Erma (sister), 8, 12, 23, 48, 86

Franklin, Vaughn (brother), 8, 10

"Freeway of Love," 93

G

Get It Right, 89

H

Hammond, John, 30–31, 39, 43

Houston, Whitney, 61, 63, 92

I

"I Knew You Were Waiting (for Me)," 94

I Never Loved a Man the Way I Love You (album), 49

"I Never Loved a Man (the Way I Love You)," (song), 45–46, 48, 49

"I Say a Little Prayer," 64

J

Jackson, Jesse, 87

Jackson, Mahalia, 6, 11, 18, 65, 68, 91

death of, 76, 79

K

King, Carole, 63–64

King, Jo, 30, 34

King, Dr. Martin Luther, Jr., 60, 65–68

L

Lady Soul, 63

Lennox, Annie, 61, 93
Love All the Hurt Away, 89

M

Mardin, Arif, 89
Mayfield, Curtis, 63, 81
Michael, George, 61, 94
Moore, Lola, 17
Motown Records, 29, 34

R

Redding, Otis, 49, 79
"Respect," 5, 49–52, 53, 57, 63, 99
Rock and Roll Hall of Fame, 7, 35, 94
"Rose Is Still a Rose, A," 102

S

secular music, 32–33
Sing, Mahalia, Sing, 91
"Sisters Are Doin' It for Themselves," 93–94
"Something He Can Feel," 81
Soul '69, 71
Southern Christian Leadership Council (SCLC), 60, 65, 67
Sparkle, 81
Supremes, the, 29, 34, 51

T

Temptations, the, 29, 51
"Think," 5, 64, 85, 103
This Girl's in Love with You, 73

Time magazine, 35, 68, 70, 84
"Today I Sing the Blues," 30–34
Turman, Glynn (husband), 82, 83–84, 85, 87, 90

U

Unforgettable: A Tribute to Dinah Washington, 40

V

Vandross, Luther, 89–90

W

Walden, Narada Michael, 92
Ward, Clara, and the Ward Singers, 6, 18–19, 20, 29, 36, 79
Warwick, Dionne, 64, 88
Washington, Dinah, 11, 32–33, 36, 39
Wexler, Jerry, 43, 45, 46, 48, 49, 65, 75, 76, 80, 85
White, Ted (husband), 36–37, 43, 46–47, 63, 68, 69, 70, 71–73, 74, 83
White, Ted Jr. (son), 37, 71, 90
Who's Zoomin' Who?, 92
Wonder, Stevie, 29, 103

Y

"(You Make Me Feel Like) A Natural Woman," 63–64
Young, Gifted and Black, 79

About the Author

Ursula Rivera was born and raised in New York City. She has been writing about celebrities for several years.

Photo Credits

Cover, pp. 4, 5, 7, 24, 70, 72, 78, 86, 88, 93, 96 © Corbis; pp. 8, 19, 28, 30, 38, 58–59 © Hulton/Archive/Getty Images; pp. 21, 22, 100–101 © AP/World Wide Photos; pp. 40, 42, 44, 49, 54, 56, 62 © Michaels Ochs Archive.

Editor

Eliza Berkowitz

Series Design

Tom Forget

Layout

Nelson Sá